Original title:
The Frozen Sun

Copyright © 2024 Swan Charm
All rights reserved.

Author: Daisy Dewi
ISBN HARDBACK: 978-9916-79-999-4
ISBN PAPERBACK: 978-9908-52-000-1
ISBN EBOOK: 978-9908-52-001-8

Shivering Brightness

The dawn breaks crisp and bright,
Whispers of frost in the light.
Silver webs catch the sun's eye,
A gentle chill in the sky.

Buds shiver in morning's embrace,
Nature's breath, a tender grace.
Colors dance on the frozen dew,
Painting dreams in a vibrant hue.

Trees stand tall, adorned in white,
Guardians of the shivering light.
Whistling winds weave through the air,
Each moment laced with winter's care.

As day unfolds and shadows play,
The brightness beckons, leads the way.
In every sparkle, hope resides,
A shivering warmth the heart provides.

Shards of Dazzling Cold

Fractured glimmers on the ground,
Each shard whispers, crisp and sound.
Crystals caught in the winter's breath,
A dance of beauty amidst the death.

Silent nights in a frosty grip,
Stars glistening, a diamond trip.
Moonlight spills like liquid glass,
In the cold, moments shatter and pass.

Frozen lakes mirror the skies,
Reflecting dreams where silence lies.
Echoes of laughter on the breeze,
Glinting fragments bring hearts to ease.

Wanderers tread on sparkling trails,
Stories written in frostbitten tales.
Each step a memory to hold,
Within the shards of dazzling cold.

The Cold Fire

Beneath the winter's starlit dome,
A cold fire beckons, calls you home.
Its warmth is felt in the heart's core,
A flicker that whispers of something more.

Snowflakes swirl in the night air,
Each a secret, a frozen prayer.
They catch the glow, they dance and swirl,
In the embrace of winter's pearl.

Crackling embers, soft and low,
Stories of hearts that long to glow.
Within the chill, a flame ignites,
Guiding souls through silent nights.

As shadows stretch and wander wide,
The cold fire stands, a steadfast guide.
In each flicker, a promise stirs,
To warm the soul as the cold blurs.

Balmy Glints Amidst Frost

In the hush of a winter day,
Balmy glints find their way.
Dancing lightly on crystal streams,
They breathe life into fading dreams.

Frosty paths, a gentle quilt,
With every glint, new warmth is built.
Glorious sun, a tender touch,
Waking the world that sleeps so much.

Underneath the icy veil,
Life awaits, in quiet scale.
Soft reflections of light's embrace,
In the heart, winter finds its place.

Through the chill, a promise flows,
In balmy glints, the soft truth grows.
Every moment, a spark divine,
Amidst the frost, hope intertwines.

Reflecting Chills

In shadows deep, the cold winds sigh,
Frosty whispers drift and fly.
The moonlight bathes the snow in sheen,
A frozen world, serene and keen.

Each breath released meets icy air,
Silent echoes, memories rare.
The night extends, a pallid cloak,
Each step a ghost, each laugh a joke.

Beneath the stars, the chill ignites,
In winter's heart, forgotten nights.
The frost's embrace, a tender hold,
A secret story, softly told.

Aurora in a Frozen Veil

Dancing lights on the horizon's edge,
Colors spill like a painter's pledge.
Whispers of the dawn softly call,
As ice holds dreams within its thrall.

Rays of warmth in a bitter chill,
Awakening wonder on the hill.
Nature's canvas, a sight so grand,
Beauty sparked by magic's hand.

Frozen shards reflect the glow,
Amply dressed in a radiant show.
Under the watch of a muted sky,
In icy stillness, the spirits fly.

Glimmering Casket of Ice

Trapped within, each crystal gleams,
A treasure hoard of frozen dreams.
Time encased in a brittle shell,
Whispers of stories it cannot tell.

The surface sparkles with silent hymns,
Nature's art in chilly whims.
A glimmer here, a flicker there,
Awakening wonder in the air.

Each shard holds whispers of the past,
Moments captured, forever cast.
In this casket, life's tales reside,
Wrapped in beauty, forever tied.

Shimmering Stillness

Glistening quiet, a sacred pause,
Nature's breath within the cause.
Every flake, a dream unfurled,
In winter's clutch, a hush is swirled.

Trees stand tall in icy crowns,
A kingdom draped in silvery gowns.
Beneath the frost, the earth holds tight,
Waiting for spring, the return of light.

Shadows dance in the fading glow,
A symphony soft, fall's final bow.
In this moment, time feels right,
In shimmering stillness, hearts take flight.

Pale Vestiges

Faded whispers in the night,
Shadows dance in the pale light.
Footsteps trace a silent path,
Echoes linger of the past.

Ghostly forms of what once lived,
Memories that time has giv'd.
Faded dreams and hollow sighs,
Lost in the veils of goodbyes.

Veins of time, they crawl and creep,
Harvesting the dreams we keep.
In the stillness, they reside,
Pale vestiges cannot hide.

Light of dawn begins to spill,
Faint hopes rise upon the chill.
Yet the past remains afloat,
In whispers, memories wrote.

Misty moments brush the air,
Ghostly echoes everywhere.
Faded yet, they still exist,
Pale vestiges that can't resist.

Eternal Frost

Winter's breath, a chilling sight,
Blankets white, the stars ignite.
Silent nights and frozen trees,
Whispers carried by the breeze.

Crystal shards that catch the glow,
In the moonlight, spirits flow.
Time stands still beneath the frost,
In this realm, we count the cost.

Frozen rivers, silent streams,
In the night, the heart still dreams.
Eternal frost, a lover's plight,
Wrapped in shivers, lost in light.

Icy tendrils weave the night,
In their grasp, we seek the bright.
Yet within the cold's embrace,
Hope ignites, a warming grace.

Through the chill, the warmth will break,
Sunrise promises to awake.
Yet for now, we drift and sway,
In eternal frost, we stay.

Captive Illumination

In the dark, a spark ignites,
Trapped within the shadowed sights.
Glimmers dance on weary walls,
Hope defies and softly calls.

Captured light in a fragile cage,
Yearning for a brighter stage.
Flickers tease the heavy gloom,
In this heart, a restless bloom.

Walls of doubt, they close in tight,
Yet the fire, it seeks the night.
Blindfolded by the fear of fate,
Hope will stir, though it's late.

Flames that flicker, softly sway,
Wings of dreams that long to play.
Caged but fierce, this heart will fight,
Yearning still for endless light.

Illumination, bittersweet,
Captive joy in a world replete.
Journey forth, no look behind,
In captive light, the heart will find.

Chilling Orbs

In the night, they softly gleam,
Chilling orbs like whispered dreams.
Suspended high in velvet sky,
Glimmers where the secrets lie.

Every shade, a story told,
Glowing soft, yet icy cold.
Infinite in their embrace,
Stars collide in quiet space.

Cascading lights in darkened streams,
Woven tales of past moonbeams.
Chilling orbs that guide the lost,
In their light, we count the cost.

Fragments of forgotten nights,
Starlit paths, eternal flights.
Every twinkle, every gleam,
Echoes of a distant dream.

Yet beneath their quiet glow,
Chilling winds begin to blow.
In this dance, we softly sway,
Chilling orbs, they light the way.

Glacial Whispers

In the silence of the night,
Where frost kisses the ground,
Whispers of ice take flight,
Echoes of secrets profound.

Moonlight dances on the snow,
Shadows weave a silver thread,
Memories of long ago,
In glacial beauty widespread.

The cold breeze softly sighs,
Tales of ages gone by,
Stars, like diamonds, shine bright,
In this serene winter sky.

Frozen streams gently flow,
Crystals gleam in the dark,
Nature's chill is aglow,
Each breath a frozen spark.

Beneath the starry dome,
Where the icy winds roam free,
In this vast, quiet home,
We find tranquility.

Twilight in Winter's Grasp

As daylight softly fades,
Shadows stretch and grow long,
Winter's grasp, a serenade,
In the silence, we belong.

Frosted branches shimmer bright,
Beneath a velvet sky,
Colors blend in soft twilight,
As the day whispers goodbye.

Footprints crunch on powdered snow,
Every step a fleeting sound,
In this magic, we all know,
Joy and peace are tightly wound.

Stars begin their nightly dance,
Glimmers in the deepening blue,
In this glow, our hearts advance,
Chasing dreams, old and new.

The evening's breath, a gentle chill,
Caresses all who dare to stay,
Winter's heart, a tranquil thrill,
In the twilight's soft decay.

Celestial Chill

Beneath the starry night,
A breath of icy air,
The cosmos gleams with light,
In the vastness, we are rare.

Galaxies swirl in grace,
Echoes of ages past,
In this expansive space,
Frozen moments meant to last.

Comets trace a brilliant path,
Whispers of time and fate,
Amid the silence, we bathe,
In awe of the celestial state.

The chill wraps round like a clue,
Connecting us to the skies,
Each twinkle speaks anew,
Of wonders we seek with our eyes.

In this cosmic embrace,
Where stars and silence meet,
We find the endless space,
Where winter's chill feels sweet.

Spheres of Subzero Light

In a realm of icy glow,
Spheres of light dance around,
Each flicker, a brilliant show,
In winter's embrace profound.

Radiant colors intertwine,
Beneath the frozen sky,
Bubbles of warmth, they align,
As cold winds gently sigh.

Gelid orbs float above,
Casting shadows on the ground,
In this spectacle of love,
Where frosty dreams are found.

With each pulse, the spheres ignite,
Revealing secrets untold,
In the dark of the night,
We witness the magic unfold.

A chilling harmony sings,
As the world turns to white,
In these subzero rings,
Winter shines, a pure delight.

Cold Light's Sweet Surrender

In the hush of silver glow,
Frosty whispers start to flow.
Gentle dawn with tender grace,
Embrace the world in soft embrace.

Nature breathes a sigh of peace,
As shadows melt, their hold does cease.
Crisp air dances in the morn,
Where dreams are stitched and hope is born.

Beneath the blanket, soft and white,
Hearts awaken to the light.
Each shimmer holds a story dear,
In cold light's warmth, there's naught to fear.

Timid blooms in icy beds,
Find their courage, lift their heads.
In the stillness, beauty sways,
Awaits the warmth of longer days.

Fleeting moments, soft and bright,
Cold light turns to sweet delight.
In surrender's gentle peace,
Life unfolds, and worries cease.

Requiem of the Winter Star

Beneath the night, a star does weep,
Its silver tears, the dreams we keep.
A chilly sigh across the sky,
In winter's grip, the echoes lie.

Frosted whispers cloud the air,
A lullaby of frost laid bare.
The quiet moon, she casts her glow,
On silent tales of ebb and flow.

Stars align with distant pain,
In shadows cast, a love remains.
The chill embraces every heart,
A fleeting warmth, yet torn apart.

In silver light, the memories gleam,
A silent world wrapped in a dream.
Beneath the shroud, the stories fade,
In winter's grasp, our hopes are laid.

Lull the song of winter's breath,
A requiem for love, for death.
Yet in the cold, the spirit flies,
And meets the warmth beyond the skies.

Dappled Illumination in Frost

Sunrise drapes the world in light,
Frosty jewels, a pure delight.
Softly glistening on the trees,
Nature's mirror, caught in freeze.

Shadows play in dappled hue,
A canvas bright, yet cold and new.
Each branch holds secrets, frozen tight,
While morning whispers, takes its flight.

Footsteps crunch on earth so bright,
In warming rays, hearts feel the light.
Sparkling crystals, a fleeting dance,
In rest's embrace, we find our chance.

Gentle winds caress the boughs,
Nature bows and takes her vows.
In the chill, life slowly stirs,
A symphony that gently purrs.

Dappled light in frosty morn,
In each heartbeat, warmth reborn.
Amidst the cold, the soul still glows,
In dazzling peace, the spirit flows.

Frigid Twinkle

Stars in the dark, their twinkle bright,
Frigid whispers in the night.
Each glance a promise, a fleeting spark,
Guiding dreams through winter's dark.

Brittle branches, etched in ice,
An artful touch, so cold, so nice.
The world adorned in shimmering gloom,
Is cradled close, as shadows loom.

Breath of frost upon the earth,
Silent songs of silent mirth.
In fleeting moments, time stands still,
As night descends with a tender thrill.

Glistening paths where shadows tread,
In every step, the stars are spread.
Frigid air that bites the skin,
Yet hearts ignite, and warmth begins.

Twinkle softly, winter's light,
Embrace the chill, the stars ignite.
In frigid realms where wonder lies,
Life dances on beneath the skies.

Frostfire's Lament

In shadows deep, the embers fade,
A chilling breath, the warmth betrayed.
Silent cries from icy ground,
Where hope and flame can't be found.

Whispers of past in the wintry air,
Hearts once bright, now laid bare.
A flicker lost, a dream well spent,
In frost and fire, souls lament.

Echoes dance on frozen streams,
Frostfire flickers in muted dreams.
The twilight's grip, a bittersweet kiss,
In the hollow night, we yearn for bliss.

Yet through the haze, a spark may start,
Hope's gentle flame ignites the heart.
In darkest times, a vision rare,
To rise anew from cold despair.

So let the frost and fire entwine,
In every struggle, strength we find.
While laments echo in winter's hold,
We forge our paths, both brave and bold.

Frigid Horizon

Beyond the glimmer of pale skies,
The frigid horizon quietly lies.
Whispers of snow on the distant crest,
Where memories wander, longing for rest.

Stars like diamonds in velvet night,
Glimpse a world devoid of light.
In solitude, the cold winds call,
A frozen echo that blankets all.

The breath of winter, sharp and clear,
Brings tales of longing, wrapped in fear.
Each frozen tear, a story told,
In silence wrapped, a heart of cold.

But deeper still, beneath the ice,
A flicker stirs, a dream unspliced.
In winter's grasp, we search for dawn,
To break the chill and carry on.

So gaze upon that distant line,
Where cold and warmth intertwine.
A horizon waits, steadfast and true,
For hearts that blossom, anew in blue.

Cold Light's Embrace

In the shimmer of morning dew,
Cold light spreads, a gentle hue.
It dances softly, veils of gray,
Caressing earth as night gives way.

Shadows linger, reluctant to flee,
Yet cold light promises to see.
Each ray a whisper, serene, profound,
In its embrace, lost warmth is found.

Lonely trees, branches entwined,
In frosty breath, their dreams aligned.
With every glimmer, a tale unfolds,
Of whispered secrets in the cold.

The world awakes to silvered skies,
Where winter's song gently sighs.
A quiet peace crowns the day,
In cold light's arms, we find our way.

Through trials faced, we persevere,
In each moment, clarity near.
Cold light shines, a guide, a muse,
In its embrace, we dare to choose.

Shattering of Warmth

When warmth shatters in the night,
Fragments fall, a muted fight.
Echoes linger in the air,
Of golden days replaced by despair.

Fractured memories fill the frost,
In fleeting touches, we pay the cost.
Hearts once bold, now wearied by cold,
The shattering echo, a tale retold.

Seeking solace in the shadows,
Hope's bright flicker, a timid glow.
In the embrace of chilly winds,
We find the strength to begin again.

Through crackling ice and distant stars,
We gather light from scattered scars.
Each broken piece, a path to grace,
In winter's grasp, we find our place.

So rise, dear heart, from warmth's retreat,
In shattered moments, we are complete.
With every fragment, love reborn,
In the cold, we greet the dawn.

Luminous Silence

In whispers soft, the night unfolds,
A tapestry of dreams in gold.
The moonlight casts a silver hue,
In luminous silence, I find you.

Stars blink gently in the sky,
While shadows dance, they softly sigh.
Each breath of night, a sacred sound,
In this quiet space, love is found.

Crickets sing their evening song,
Echoes of peace where we belong.
A heart's embrace in twilight's glow,
In luminous silence, feelings flow.

Wrapped in warmth of the night's caress,
Time stands still, a sweet finesse.
The world outside seems far away,
In tranquil moments, we drift and sway.

Together here, in softest light,
Where memories linger in the night.
A bond that grows, the stars align,
In luminous silence, your heart is mine.

Starlit Freeze

Underneath the velvet sky,
The starlit freeze catches the eye.
Crystals twinkle, bright and clear,
Awakening dreams that come so near.

Footprints crunch on frosted ground,
In this stillness, love is found.
The world transformed by winter's art,
A starlit freeze that warms the heart.

Winds whisper secrets through the trees,
As night unravels, cool and free.
Each breath a cloud, a fleeting sight,
In starlit freeze, we chase the night.

Laughter echoes, spirits soar,
As joy and wonder we explore.
Under stars that softly gleam,
In starlit freeze, we share a dream.

So hold my hand, let's take a chance,
In the quiet, our hearts dance.
Together wrapped in nature's ease,
In this moment, starlit freeze.

A Dance of Ice and Glow

In the heart of winter's bite,
Frosty breaths ignite the night.
A dance of ice upon the floor,
With every step, we crave for more.

Through shimmering paths, we glide and spin,
In the chill, warm sparks within.
The firelight flickers, shadows grow,
As we revel in this ice and glow.

Each twirl and laugh, a fleeting sigh,
Under the vast and starry sky.
In glistening snow, our spirits soar,
In a dance of ice, forevermore.

With every moment, your hand in mine,
Together lost in warmth divine.
The world fades out, in gentle flow,
As we weave our tale in this glow.

Embrace the magic, let us flow,
In this shimmering world, love will grow.
A fleeting night, let the music know,
In a dance of ice and glow.

Frosted Memories

In winter's hold, the world is still,
Frosted memories, time to fill.
With every breath, the past begins,
In icy dreams where love still wins.

Gold and silver, a painted sky,
Where echoes of laughter drift and fly.
Each flake that falls, a story told,
In frosted memories, hearts unfold.

Captured moments in the gleam,
Soft whispers of a distant dream.
Through tangled branches, the sun breaks through,
In frost-kissed beauty, I see you.

Time slips softly, a gentle glide,
Embracing warmth, our hearts collide.
In every shimmer, our tale remains,
In frosted memories, joy sustains.

So let's carve out our dreams anew,
In this winter, just me and you.
With each heartbeat, let love flow,
In frosted memories, forever grow.

Sunbeams in a Crystal World

In the morning's gentle light,
Sunbeams dance on snowy white.
Each glimmer tells a secret tale,
Of winter's charm, so pure and frail.

Trees adorned with sparkling grace,
Nature's jewels in every space.
A world transformed, so bright and clear,
Awakens wonder, draws us near.

Shadows play beneath the glow,
Whispers from the earth below.
In this realm where magic swirls,
We find the beauty of our worlds.

The air is crisp, the heart shall soar,
As sunbeams weave forevermore.
A crystal world, both vast and deep,
Embracing dreams that softly seep.

In every flake, in every beam,
We catch a glimpse of nature's dream.
With open hearts, we wander free,
In sunlit realms, just you and me.

Radiant Frost

Silver layers greet the morn,
As frosty breath on earth is worn.
Each crystal spark, a fleeting sight,
A symphony of cold and light.

Across the fields, a shimmer spreads,
Nature's quilt on which time treads.
With every step, the crunch beneath,
Awakens life, dispels the grief.

The world transformed in icy grace,
A tranquil hush, a sacred space.
In frozen beauty, hearts unite,
In radiant frost, we find our light.

The sun ascends, the chill retreats,
A dance of warmth that softly greets.
Yet memories of winter's show,
Will linger long in hearts aglow.

As shadows fade and daylight beams,
We carry forth our winter dreams.
A fleeting touch, a whispered thought,
In radiant frost, our souls are caught.

The Quiet Blaze

In twilight's hush, the fires glow,
A quiet blaze, so soft and slow.
Each flicker speaks of warmth and light,
In the embrace of lingering night.

Shadows weave upon the walls,
As evening's gentle silence falls.
We gather close, with hearts aflame,
In whispered words, we share our names.

The dance of flames, a tender song,
In every heart where we belong.
Rich embers flicker, bright and clear,
Call us forth, our stories near.

With every spark, a memory glows,
A tapestry of love that grows.
In the quiet, in the haze,
We find our peace in the quiet blaze.

So let us sit, let spirits rise,
Underneath the starlit skies.
In unity, our souls embrace,
Forever bound in the quiet blaze.

Polar Dawn

In the stillness of the morn,
Polar dawn is gently born.
Colors burst in soft array,
As night gives in to blushing day.

Frosted lands begin to gleam,
Awakening from winter's dream.
Each breath of air, a new delight,
In the magic of pure light.

Crystals crackle underfoot,
Where shadows dance and silence soot.
A fleeting warmth spreads through the chill,
As dawn unfolds with grace and will.

Mountains rise in rugged bold,
With secrets of the night retold.
In every gleam, in every hue,
The polar dawn calls out to you.

As day breaks forth in vibrant glow,
We find the strength in what we know.
In nature's arms, our spirits drawn,
Forever blessed by polar dawn.

Winter's Perpetual Light

Frosty breath on a silvery dawn,
Branches shimmer like diamonds, drawn.
Whispers of snowflakes gently fall,
Covering earth in a glistening shawl.

Shadows stretch with the lengthening day,
While sunlight dances, chasing gray.
Every corner glows with pure delight,
In the soft warmth of winter's light.

Crisp air carries a melody sweet,
Echoing laughter on snow-covered street.
Children play, their joy in flight,
Embracing the charm of winter's light.

The sky wears a canvas painted in blue,
Where dreams mingle with the frosty dew.
Nature whispers, soft and bright,
Inviting all to behold the sight.

Evening falls with a twilight sigh,
Stars emerge in the starlit sky.
Under its gaze, we find respite,
Wrapped in warmth of winter's light.

Hidden Fire of Frost

Underneath the icy shield,
A warmth of life can be revealed.
Beneath the surface, embers glow,
A hidden fire beneath the snow.

Crystals form with a silent grace,
Enveloping all in a frosty embrace.
Yet in this chill, a spark ignites,
Fueling dreams on starry nights.

Breath of winter, crisp and clear,
Whispers of what we hold dear.
In every flake, a tale reborn,
From grayish dusk to rosy morn.

Twilight hovers, painting the skies,
As twilight's blush softly lies.
Within the cold, the heart beats bright,
In the hidden fire of frost's delight.

In the heart of winter, we seek the flame,
Nurtured warmth, we call its name.
With every breath, we'll choose to fight,
For love abides in hidden light.

Sterling Blaze

Moonlight casts a silver hue,
Draping the world in a tranquil view.
With every step, the crisp snow sighs,
As shadows dance beneath the skies.

Stars twinkle like jewels bright,
Guiding the way with gentle light.
The night whispers secrets untold,
In the calm of winter, bold and cold.

A hint of fire beneath the chill,
Burning softly, it lingers still.
In the heart's warmth, all feels right,
Bathed in the glow of the sterling night.

Each breath we take draws us close,
In the silver veil, we find our prose.
Together we stand, hearts ablaze,
In the cold, we find our praise.

The dawn approaches, a brighter day,
With every moment, come what may.
In winter's grasp, the spirit plays,
Embracing the warmth of sterling blaze.

Harmony of Ice and Light

Glistening snowflakes twirl and sway,
Creating art in a cold ballet.
Where the sun kisses the frozen ground,
A harmony of ice and light is found.

Trees stand tall, dressed in white,
Reflecting all with a stunning sight.
The air is crisp, a sweet delight,
Carrying songs of pure insight.

In twilight's embrace, colors merge,
The world awash with a subtle surge.
Every moment feels just right,
In the dance of ice and light.

With hearts aglow, we share this space,
In winter's realm, a warm embrace.
Together, we traverse the bright,
Finding solace in the night.

As starlight weaves through frozen trees,
We revel in nature's quiet ease.
In this season, we feel the height,
Of peace found in harmony of ice and light.

Beyond the Snowy Horizon

The mountains rise, so grand and white,
A canvas spread, in soft daylight.
Whispers of wind, in silence speak,
Footprints lost, where the wild things seek.

Frosted trees, like ghosts they stand,
Guardians of this frozen land.
In the distance, echoes call,
A distant dream, too far for all.

The sun dips low, in hues of fire,
Painting skies, with heart's desire.
Beyond the waves of glistening snow,
Lies a beauty few ever know.

Stars awaken, in velvet veil,
Guiding travelers, who dare to sail.
Through the chill and the moon's embrace,
They wander on, a timeless chase.

Beneath the icy grip of night,
Life stirs gently, hidden from sight.
In the stillness, a heartbeat flows,
Beyond the line where the adventure grows.

Whisper of a Solar Mirage

Beneath the sun, the sands do gleam,
A mirage forms, like a fleeting dream.
Rippling heat, it dances bright,
In the distance, out of sight.

Whispers float on the heated air,
Secrets shared without a care.
Waves of shimmer, lose their grace,
Life reflected in a sunlit space.

An oasis calls, a siren's song,
Tempting weary souls to roam along.
But reality, it fades away,
Leaving shadows where visions play.

Colors blend in a vibrant swirl,
Nature paints as the breezes twirl.
Through the haze, a flicker glows,
A world beyond, that only one knows.

Yet, as the day begins to wane,
The mirage dies, leaving but a stain.
The sun sets low, in fiery embrace,
A tender kiss upon the face.

Celestial Freeze

In the night, a blanket spread,
Stars like diamonds, overhead.
Galaxies swirl in cosmic dance,
Inviting all to take a chance.

Cold winds whisper tales of old,
Secrets wrapped in icy hold.
The moon, a lantern, softly glows,
Illuminating shadows' throes.

Frozen lakes, like glass they gleam,
Reflecting dreams, a lucid beam.
In this stillness, time suspends,
A moment swallowed, never ends.

Howling winds, they weave a thread,
Telling stories of those long dead.
Among the stars, their spirits roam,
Finding peace in the celestial dome.

Embrace the night, the chill so pure,
In the cosmic arms, we find our cure.
For in the freeze, life takes a pause,
A whispered sigh, with no applause.

Timeless Chill

Amidst the frost, the silence reigns,
Crafting beauty, where stillness gains.
Winter's breath, a gentle sigh,
Painting frost on the close-pie sky.

Every flake, a story spun,
Dances lightly, from moon to sun.
In the air, a crisp allure,
A fragile moment, bold and pure.

Footprints linger on paths of white,
Tracing dreams in the soft moonlight.
Each step whispers of days gone by,
In the silence, memories lie.

A chill runs deep, through forest tall,
Echoes of nature's timeless call.
Among the trees, wise secrets flow,
In this embrace, the heartbeats grow.

As dawn approaches, the glow unfurls,
Shattering dreams in frost-covered swirls.
Yet, in the chill, a warmth endures,
With love's soft touch, the heart ensures.

Awash in Feathery White

A blanket lies upon the ground,
Soft whispers all around me sound.
Each flake dances, a graceful flight,
Weaving dreams in the purest white.

Trees adorned with icy lace,
Nature's canvas, a tranquil space.
Footsteps crunch, a crisp delight,
In this hush, the world feels right.

Breathe in deep this frosty air,
With every sigh, release a care.
The chill enchants, a gentle bite,
Wrapped in warmth, hearts feel light.

Candles flicker in twilight's glow,
Casting shadows, soft and slow.
In this moment, peace ignites,
Awash in feathery white delights.

As daylight fades and stars emerge,
Silence stirs, a mystic surge.
In moonlit grace, spirits take flight,
Lost in dreams of the night so bright.

Sparking the Silent Chia

A tiny seed within my palm,
Yearns for water, wakes in calm.
With love, I cradle softly tight,
Sparking life, a joyful sight.

Gentle sprout begins to rise,
Reaching upward toward the skies.
Each leaf unfurls with pure delight,
Transforming shadows into light.

Nature whispers through each vein,
Life unfolds in joy and pain.
With tender care, it grows so bright,
In silent mornings, pure and right.

Morning dew, a jeweled crown,
Glittering where green is found.
The world awakes, fresh and bright,
Sparking hope in each daylight.

As seasons shift and moments fade,
Life's experiments we've all made.
In every heart, a tiny light,
Sparking the silent chia's flight.

A Promise of Warmth

In the hearth where embers glow,
Whispers dance, their secrets flow.
Underneath a quilted night,
A promise lingers, pure and bright.

Cups of cocoa, rich and sweet,
Gather 'round, where lovers meet.
In shared laughter, hearts ignite,
A promise of warmth, holding tight.

Snowflakes fall like whispered dreams,
Each one holds a thousand themes.
With every sip, the world feels right,
Wrapped in love, a warm invite.

Stars above, a twinkling sight,
Hearts entwined, souls take flight.
Through every trial, every plight,
A promise of warmth in silent night.

When the winds howl fierce and cold,
In our hearts, we find the bold.
Together weaving stories bright,
A promise of warmth, our guiding light.

Suspended Radiance

In twilight's embrace, we find our peace,
Gentle hues that never cease.
Whispers of gold in the fading light,
Suspended radiance, pure delight.

Through branches bare the sunlight streams,
Shimmering softly, like fleeting dreams.
Each moment captured, a fleeting sight,
In this canvas, beauty ignites.

Silhouettes dance against the sky,
As colors swirl and gently sigh.
In the balance of day and night,
Suspended radiance, a heart's delight.

The horizon blurs, a softened line,
Where time stands still, and stars align.
Drenched in wonder, every height,
Suspended radiance, purest light.

Embrace the magic, let it flow,
In every heartbeat, love will grow.
For in this moment, held so tight,
Suspended radiance, life ignites.

When Light Meets Ice

In the stillness, shadows glide,
A whisper of warmth, a soft tide.
Light dances on frozen ground,
In this moment, peace is found.

Crystals shimmer, break the night,
Reflecting dreams, pure and bright.
Beneath the winter's cold embrace,
Hope flickers in this tranquil space.

A symphony of silence sings,
As the world pauses, gently clings.
To the beauty of winter's grace,
Where time slows in icy lace.

Each breath, a ghost in the air,
The chill is sharp, yet we don't care.
For in the light, we see the spark,
That warms our hearts against the dark.

So let us wander, hand in hand,
In a landscape, vast and grand.
Where light meets ice in soft delight,
And fills our souls with purest light.

Frigid Luminescence

Stars appear in velvet skies,
Twinkling dreams and whispered sighs.
Moonbeams chase the ghosts of night,
Guiding travelers with soft light.

Through the trees, a silver glow,
Casts shadows deep upon the snow.
Crystalline breath hangs in the air,
A dance of frost, both bold and rare.

Each flake unique, a fleeting gem,
In this frozen diadem.
We marvel at the beauty found,
In winter's whisper, pure and sound.

The world rests in a tranquil hush,
As time flows by, a gentle rush.
In the stillness, life is bright,
A canvas brushed in purest white.

And so we stand beneath the glow,
Feeling warmth in winter's flow.
Frigid luminescence calls,
As the heart hears winter's palls.

The Winter's Hearth

Amidst the cold, a fire burns bright,
Crackling softly, a warm delight.
Surrounded by shadows, we gather near,
Sharing tales, the laughter clear.

The hearth glows with a golden hue,
Illuminating faces, a cozy crew.
Outside, the world is draped in white,
Inside, we find purest night.

Winter's breath kisses frosted glass,
While embers dance, as moments pass.
In this refuge, worries cease,
As time unfolds in warmth and peace.

Snowflakes swirl in the quiet breeze,
Nature's art on sleeping trees.
Yet here, we find a vibrant heart,
A tapestry where warmth imparts.

With every sip, the chill dissolves,
In laughter, love, the soul evolves.
Together we breathe in the mirth,
United in joy, around the hearth.

Sunlight in the Ice

Golden rays through frosted pines,
Creating patterns, nature's designs.
A prism of colors, sharp and clear,
Whispers of warmth, drawing us near.

In frozen realms where shadows play,
Sunlight dances, a sweet ballet.
Each glimmer, a promise of spring,
A soft reminder of life's sweet fling.

The world adorned in sparkling coats,
Where silence sings and winter floats.
With every beam, hope starts to rise,
Painting dreams in morning skies.

A touch of warmth on chilly skin,
Inviting smiles, the spark within.
For even in cold, hearts can ignite,
Finding comfort in purest light.

And as the day gives way to night,
We carry forth the day's warm bite.
In the memory of ice and sun,
We find the joy in what's begun.

Crystal Halo

In the forest's quiet dome,
A shimmering light begins to roam.
Soft whispers of the night,
Beneath stars shining bright.

A halo formed of crystal grace,
Reflects the moon's gentle face.
With each step, magic flows,
In the air, enchantment glows.

The branches weave a sparkling net,
Where dreams and reality softly met.
Nature's jewels in the deep,
Awaken wonders long asleep.

In the stillness, shadows dance,
Inviting hearts to take a chance.
Underneath the twinkling sky,
The soul learns to soar and fly.

A promise hangs on each cool breath,
And leads us gently towards the depth.
Through the glimmer, we shall find,
The light that glows within the mind.

Frosted Illumination

In silver dawn, the world aglow,
Each flake of frost begins to show.
Beneath the brightening sky,
The shimmering wonder brings a sigh.

Through branches draped in icy lace,
The sun emerges, a warm embrace.
Each crystal sparkles, tells a tale,
Of winter's grace where dreams prevail.

Winds whisper softly, secrets spin,
As frosted hues invite us in.
With every breath, a shimmering art,
Nature and magic laid apart.

Upon the ground, a canvas white,
The earth transforms in soft daylight.
In this moment, hearts ignite,
With every shadow, pure delight.

Through frosted paths that twist and weave,
The spirit dances, learns to believe.
Illumination in every glance,
As winter unfolds her tender romance.

Ethereal Chill

In midnight's hush, cool breezes sigh,
The world beneath a starlit sky.
An ethereal chill wraps around,
Where whispers of magic can be found.

Soft shadows blend with silver light,
Nature's beauty in the night.
Each breath a cloud, so soft and white,
Carried on waves of dreams taking flight.

The moon's glow paints the earth anew,
In shades of blue and gleaming hue.
A tranquil peace, a calming thrill,
In every heart, the winter's chill.

Through mystic woods, the spirits roam,
In every corner, they find a home.
Ethereal laughter, echoes near,
As night unfolds, we hold it dear.

Beneath the gaze of timeless stars,
We find the magic, near and far.
In stillness, we embrace the thrill,
Forever touched by the ethereal chill.

Bound by Ice

A frozen land where silence speaks,
In icy realms, the spirit seeks.
Mountains stand with resolute grace,
Time is captured in this place.

Beneath the surface, stories lie,
Of days gone past, like whispered sighs.
Each shard of ice a tale conceals,
Of ancient wounds, and hope that heals.

Across the landscape, shadows play,
As twilight leads the night astray.
A canvas brushed with hues of frost,
Where every moment feels embossed.

In winter's clasp, we often pause,
To hear the nature's quiet laws.
Every flake a piece of art,
Bound by ice, yet close to heart.

Through glistening trails of white we tread,
With every step, old fears are shed.
In unity, with the frigid space,
Bound by ice, we find our place.

Surreal Planetshine

In twilight's grip, the worlds collide,
Stars express what dreams confide.
Colors swirl in cosmic dance,
Caught in fate's mysterious trance.

Whispers drift on zephyr's breath,
Echoes of a long-lost quest.
Galaxies in silence weep,
As secrets of the night creep.

Beneath the glow of azure skies,
Time unravels, softly sighs.
Minds ignite in realms unknown,
In this space we are alone.

Crimson trails and silver streams,
Reality is stitched from dreams.
Floating free, we find our way,
Chasing shadows till the day.

A tapestry of light unfurls,
In every heart, a galaxy twirls.
Surreal beauty found in flight,
Awaking souls to endless night.

The Icy Embrace of Dawn

A fragile veil in morning's grace,
Whispers soft in time and space.
Frosted branches, diamonds glow,
Winter's breath begins to show.

The world awakes with gentle cries,
Chasing dreams beneath pale skies.
Sunrise spills its golden tears,
Warming hearts and calming fears.

In shadows long, the chill remains,
Echoes of past's bittersweet chains.
Each breath a mist, a fleeting sign,
Of nature's pulse, a sacred line.

Birds ascend, their songs take wing,
Dancing on the breeze of spring.
Hope reborn in every hue,
In icy clasp, we find what's true.

Awake, arise, the day is young,
Life's melody yet to be sung.
In dawn's embrace, we stand anew,
In this light, we find our view.

Mirth in the Midnight Frost

Moonlit laughter fills the air,
In the frost, we lose our care.
Stars above like diamonds twine,
In the chill, our spirits shine.

A dance of shadows, wild and free,
Echoes of our jubilee.
Joy ignites in winter's hush,
Underneath the frosty brush.

Footprints etched on glistening ground,
In the silence, magic found.
Each step whispers tales untold,
Wrapped in warmth amidst the cold.

Hearts entwined in starlit cheer,
Moments treasured, drawing near.
In laughter's grip, we break the night,
Mirth that glows in silver light.

With every breath, the world feels new,
In the frost, there's joy for two.
Boundless joy in the midnight's reign,
In every heartbeat, love's refrain.

Breaths of Shimmering Cold

A breath released, a shimmer bright,
In the cold, we chase the light.
Crystal edges catch the dawn,
Nature whispers, gently drawn.

In frosty air, the promise speaks,
Of warmth that under winter peaks.
Each sigh a story, soft and clear,
In winter's grip, we find our cheer.

Through glades of white, the shadows play,
Painting paths along the way.
As daylight breaks, our hopes unfold,
In every breath, the world feels bold.

The icy weave of time entwined,
In sparkling moments, dreams aligned.
A symphony of stillness sings,
Embracing all that nature brings.

With every pulse, the cold ignites,
Awakening in frosted nights.
Together here, our spirits soar,
In breaths of cold, we crave for more.

Crystalized Hues

In quiet shades, the colors gleam,
Frosted whispers in a dream.
Crystals dance on winter's breath,
Painting beauty, braving death.

A palette formed from nature's grace,
Every hue a soft embrace.
Reflecting light in gentle waves,
A world transformed, the silence saves.

Beneath the frost, old stories lie,
Tales of love that never die.
In every shard, a memory sings,
Of summer days and other things.

As twilight dims the day's warm glow,
Crystalized hues begin to show.
Each facet holds a fleeting spark,
A timeless beauty, bold yet stark.

In frozen realms where echoes dwell,
Nature's voice casts a gentle spell.
In every glimmer, truth will rise,
Beneath the weight of winter skies.

A Flicker Beyond the Ice

Beyond the frost, a light will shine,
Flickering soft, a path divine.
Each glimmer whispers tales untold,
Of realms where warmth defies the cold.

In shadowed woods, the shadows sway,
Dancing spirits in disarray.
A beacon calls through frozen night,
A flicker set against the plight.

With every pulse, the world will thaw,
Nature wakes to heed the law.
From icy grips, the life is freed,
Renewed by sparks that gently lead.

In this embrace, we find our peace,
The flicker brings a sweet release.
As firelight dims the icy veil,
Hope emerges where hearts prevail.

A journey marked by twilight's glow,
To follow where the warm winds blow.
Through shadows, we shall find the light,
A flicker bright, our souls ignite.

Solstice in Solitude

In tranquil times, the solstice rests,
A fleeting pause, nature's quests.
The longest night wraps all in care,
A silent call of dreams laid bare.

Stars above weave tales of old,
Whispers of warmth, of life retold.
Each breeze shall carry silent pleas,
A solace found amidst the trees.

In solitude, a heart can roam,
Finding in stillness a hidden home.
Where shadows play and echoes sigh,
Beneath the vast, eternal sky.

Embrace the night, let worries fade,
In solstice time, we are remade.
Through dark, we search for flints of dawn,
A promise held, a new day drawn.

Alone we stand, yet not in vain,
For from the dark, we break our chains.
In solitude, we find our way,
Through winter's grip to warmer days.

Frosted Echoes of Light

In morning's glow, the frost awakes,
Each crystal refracts, a world it makes.
Echoes of light on surfaces shine,
A frosted canvas, nature's design.

Through branches bare, the glimmers play,
Their shimmering dance sparks the day.
Each ray of sun, a soft embrace,
Frosted echoes in quiet space.

A gentle hush hangs in the air,
Moments caught, beyond compare.
Nature's voice, a whisper so clear,
Echoes of beauty, drawing near.

As daylight wanes, the colors shift,
Echoing warmth in winter's gift.
In fading light, the spirits rise,
Frosted echoes in evening skies.

So hear the call, the silent song,
In every light, we all belong.
Frosted whispers of what ignites,
In our hearts, the echoes of light.

Dusk in a White World

Quiet whispers fill the air,
Snowflakes dance without a care.
Shadows stretch across the ground,
In the stillness, peace is found.

Fading light begins to glow,
In the dusk, a soft tableau.
Crystal branches shine like dreams,
Nature wrapped in glistening beams.

Footsteps muffled, time stands still,
As the evening seeks to thrill.
Underneath a sky of gray,
Wonders linger, drift away.

Colors fade to shades of blue,
In this world, serene and true.
Moments captured, hearts ignite,
Dusk unfolding into night.

A breath of cold, a touch of peace,
In this white world, sorrows cease.
Every flake, a story spun,
Dusk in winter, all is one.

Veil of Icy Brilliance

Underneath a silver sheen,
Nature wears a crown unseen.
Every branch, a work of art,
Veil of ice that grips the heart.

Crystals shimmer in the light,
Casting magic through the night.
Frozen whispers weave a tale,
On the wind, a soft exhale.

Glistening paths of frosted dew,
Secrets held in shades of blue.
Every step, a careful grace,
In this wondrous, silent space.

Twinkling stars above us gleam,
In the stillness, we can dream.
Cold embraces, warmth inside,
In this brilliance, we confide.

A moment's pause, the world at rest,
Veil of ice, the purest quest.
Nature's artwork on display,
Brilliance shines in crisp ballet.

Silvered Light

Morning breaks with silver rays,
Chasing shadows, brightening days.
Each blade of grass, a spark of fire,
Silvered light, a soft attire.

Fields awaken, stretch and sigh,
As the sun ascends the sky.
Dewdrops cling to every stalk,
Nature sings, begins to talk.

A gentle breeze brings whispers low,
Carrying tales of long ago.
Silver streams reflect the sun,
In this moment, life's begun.

Colors bloom in vibrant hues,
Painted skies with shades of blues.
Silver light that warms the soul,
Binding nature, making whole.

Every ray, a thread of hope,
In this dance, we learn to cope.
Silvered light in morning's grace,
Fills our hearts, a warm embrace.

Radiance in Permafrost

In the cold where stillness reigns,
Beauty hides in icy veins.
Radiance in frozen space,
Mirrored worlds in time and place.

Crystalline glimmers, soft and bright,
Illuminate the velvet night.
Every snowy drift a dream,
Nature whispers, weaves a theme.

Silent echoes, winter's song,
In this realm, we all belong.
Footsteps crunch on frosty ground,
In this radiance, peace is found.

Glistening stars in velvet skies,
Reflecting hopes, like ancient sighs.
Permafrost, a canvas wide,
Where dreams and nature coincide.

Every breath, a cloud of white,
In this wonder, hearts feel light.
Radiance through the frozen mist,
In this world, we shall persist.

Wreath of Sunlit Frost

A wreath of frost upon the ground,
Sparkling in the morning light,
Nature whispers all around,
Embraced in winter's white delight.

Trees adorned in icy lace,
Glistening in the sun's warm glow,
Each branch holding its gentle grace,
A silent beauty in the snow.

Footprints trace a tale of old,
Stories hidden in the frost,
Nature's canvas, pure and bold,
In this season, nothing's lost.

The breath of chills in crisp, clear air,
Breathless moments float like dreams,
Soft whispers of a world so rare,
A tranquility that gleams.

At dusk, the hues begin to blend,
Shadows dance with waning light,
A day concludes, yet memories send,
A wreath of dusk, serene and bright.

Frost-laden Dreams

Frost-laden dreams take flight at dawn,
Carried on the winter's breeze,
Whispers of the night now gone,
Echoes through the swaying trees.

A world transformed in silver hue,
Each flake a story softly spun,
Beneath the sky of deepest blue,
Winter's dance has just begun.

The silence wraps around so tight,
A blanket soft, the earth's embrace,
In this stillness, pure delight,
A sanctuary, a sacred space.

Stars like diamonds grace the night,
Guiding dreams with twinkling beams,
Wrapped in warmth, the heart takes flight,
In slumber's hold, we chase our dreams.

As dawn arrives, the light ascends,
The glories of a new day call,
Frost-laden dreams, where magic blends,
Into the warmth, we rise, we fall.

Winter's Glimmering Veil

Under winter's glimmering veil,
Life is hushed, a quiet grace,
Each breath of cold tells a tale,
Of fleeting moments we embrace.

Softly falls the crystal snow,
Like gentle whispers from the skies,
A blanket that the earth will know,
Hiding secrets with soft sighs.

As shadows stretch and daylight fades,
The stars awaken from their sleep,
In icy fields, the world parades,
A dreamlike slumber, deep and steep.

With every flake, a wish is sent,
To travel through the night so free,
In stillness, our hearts are content,
Wrapped in the warmth of memory.

Onward flows the river's hush,
Time feels slow, yet swiftly flies,
In winter's arms, we softly blush,
As hope beneath the frost still lies.

Ethereal Chill

In the grip of ethereal chill,
Where time stands still and whispers grow,
The world outside is quiet and still,
Wrapped in blankets of silver snow.

Frosty breath on window panes,
Patterns etched in frozen lace,
Nature's art, where beauty reigns,
Capturing the light's embrace.

Footsteps crunch on paths of white,
As laughter rings through frosty air,
In winter's heart, pure joy ignites,
Moments shared with love and care.

Stars twinkle like the night's soft kiss,
Beacons in the velvet sky,
Each glimmer holds a secret wish,
That dreams and hopes will learn to fly.

Through the chill, we find our spark,
A warmth that blankets heart and soul,
In winter's grasp, where life embarks,
To dance beneath the frosted bowl.

The Shivering Radiance

In twilight's grasp, the shadows creep,
A whispering glow, secrets to keep.
Stars tremble with a silvered light,
A dance of dusk, before the night.

Flickers soft in the evening hush,
As colors fade in a gentle rush.
Silent echoes fill the vast expanse,
While dreams awaken, in twilight's trance.

Galaxies weave on fabric so deep,
Beneath a sky where shadows seep.
Each glimmering spark, a story untold,
In the heart of night, a treasure of gold.

Moonbeams spill on the troubled sea,
A ripple of light where none can flee.
With every pulse, the night does sing,
Of hopes and fears, the dawn will bring.

Yet in this glow, the cold does bite,
A contrast fierce, from dark to light.
But in that shiver, warmth may glow,
In the silent prayer of shadows slow.

When Warmth Turns to Chill

In the heart of noon, a sun's embrace,
Life dances bright in nature's face.
But whispers come, a breeze so stark,
A chill creeps in, igniting the dark.

Of laughter shared, now echoes sigh,
When warmth dissolves, we wonder why.
The laughter fades, as moments flee,
When warmth turns chill, what's left to be?

Frosted breaths on tender lips,
Delicate dreams from frigid trips.
With every turn, the world feels tight,
As shadows linger beyond the light.

Yet in the chill, resilience glows,
A quiet strength that softly grows.
We gather close, amid the frost,
What once was warm, we will not lost.

As seasons turn and rhythms shift,
In every chill, we find a gift.
For in the cold, we learn to brave,
The beauty found in every wave.

Flicker in the Glacial Night

A single star in a sea of black,
Paints the canvas with a silver track.
In icy depths, where shadows play,
A flicker whispers the night away.

Time slows down, as the clock unwinds,
In frozen moments, the heart reminds.
Each glimmer bright, a beacon of fire,
In glacial breaths, we all conspire.

The chill surrounds, but still we yearn,
For warmth that flickers, and heartbeats turn.
In every spark, a hope ignites,
Against the frost of enduring nights.

We gather strength in the cold embrace,
As dreams awaken, we find our place.
In this vast silence, a truth revealed,
A flicker shines, our fears healed.

So let us dance in this frozen light,
With every heartbeat, we reclaim the night.
In the stillness, our spirits ignite,
As flickers guide us, through the starlit sight.

Gleams of the Frosted Orb

Round and radiant in the velvet sky,
A frosted orb, where spirits fly.
Beneath its glow, the world transforms,
In shimmering dreams, the magic swarms.

With every gleam, the shadows thrill,
As hidden secrets in silence spill.
In winter's grasp, a tale unfolds,
Of whispered wishes, and hearts so bold.

The frost engraves a tapestry fine,
Of moments lost, in the vine's twine.
Each sparkle sings of night's embrace,
A dance of fate, a tender grace.

In the stillness of the midnight air,
Gleams beckon with a gentle care.
A promise wrapped in winter's shawl,
To light the way through the darkest fall.

So look above to the frosted scene,
In every flicker, a chance to glean.
For in each glow, a truth resounds,
In the orb's light, our love surrounds.

Chill of the Distant Star

A whisper travels through the night,
Cold winds carry starry light.
In silence wrapped, the cosmos sighs,
A chill that touches, never lies.

Flickers dance on velvet skies,
Each one a dream that softly flies.
The night unfolds its crystal wings,
While in the dark, the heartbeat rings.

Lost in thought, I gaze above,
A longing heart, a sigh of love.
Beneath the glow of ancient fire,
I find my thoughts, as dreams conspire.

A memory of worlds unknown,
In the chill, I feel at home.
The distant past, the future's dream,
A cosmic thread, a silver beam.

Underneath the vast expanse,
I sense the stars begin to dance.
With every flicker that I see,
The cold still warms the soul in me.

Frigid Glimmer

In frosty air, the shadows play,
At dawn's first light, they fade away.
A glimmer shines on icy ground,
Silent beauty all around.

Each breath I take, a swirling mist,
In the chill, the world's abyss.
Whispers of winter brush my cheek,
In this stillness, I feel weak.

Stars dip low, the night retreats,
Embracing cold in gentle beats.
With every ray of light that bends,
The frigid air, it softly mends.

Trees adorned in crystal white,
Shimmering softly in morning light.
A tranquil scene, serene yet bold,
Nature's canvas, pure and cold.

The glimmer fades as day awakes,
With every pulse, the silence breaks.
Yet in the heart where shadows blend,
A frigid glow will never end.

Icy Radiance

A glow emerges from the frost,
In icy realms, all warmth is lost.
Yet in the chill, a spark remains,
A radiance in icy chains.

The moonlight weaves through dormant trees,
A silver thread that teases the breeze.
With every shimmer, secrets wake,
In frozen whispers, dreams we stake.

A canvas white, untouched and pure,
In this void, my heart's allure.
Each snowflake tells a story rare,
A fleeting moment caught mid-air.

Like diamonds scattered in the night,
Each icy shard, a heart's delight.
Icy radiance illuminates,
A world transformed, it captivates.

So in the stillness, I shall roam,
From frozen paths, my heart finds home.
In every glimmer, every gaze,
An icy radiance guides my ways.

Shards of a Cold Dawn

As dawn breaks soft on frosty ground,
Shards of light begin to resound.
The world awakes in muted hues,
In icy breath, the promise brews.

Crystals clash in morning's grip,
Each tone a gentle, fleeting sip.
With every ray that starts to creep,
The night's cold touch begins to weep.

A tapestry of glimmers bright,
In the distance, the fading night.
Fractured beams in shades of blue,
Whisper secrets of thoughts anew.

The chill of dawn, a bittersweet,
With tender whispers, we repeat.
Each fragment tells of what has passed,
In shards of cold, our dreams are cast.

Yet in the freeze, there's warmth to find,
In every crack, the light is kind.
So let the morning break the spell,
In shards of dawn, we rise, we dwell.

Winter's Embrace

Snowflakes dance upon the air,
Whispers of chill everywhere.
Branches bare, a world asleep,
Silence holds the secrets deep.

Footprints trace the icy ground,
In this quiet, peace is found.
Fires crackle, warmth inside,
While the frosty winds abide.

Stars above in velvet blue,
Glisten softly, bright and true.
Nature's breath, a frosted sigh,
Winter's embrace, a lullaby.

Moonlight spills on fields so wide,
Shadows stretch where dreams reside.
In this wonder, hearts ignite,
Winter's spell, a pure delight.

So let the season take its hold,
Tales of warmth in nights so cold.
For every icy glance we find,
A cozy glow in hearts combined.

Luminous Frost

Morning glows with frosted light,
Nature dressed in purest white.
Glistening leaves reflect the dawn,
A world renewed, a beauty drawn.

Sunrise paints the sky with fire,
Cold embracing, hearts desire.
Every breath, a cloud of mist,
In this moment, magic kissed.

Footsteps crunch on frozen ground,
Whispers of wonders all around.
Branches sparkling with delight,
In luminous frosts, pure and bright.

Winter's palette, soft and pale,
Tales of seasons in the gale.
Stars retreat as day awakes,
A luminous frost, our hearts it takes.

So breathe the air, so crisp, so clear,
In this moment, hold it dear.
For every chill, a warmth will rise,
In the glow of winter skies.

Shimmering Shadows

Beneath the moon's ethereal glow,
Shadows dance in depths of snow.
Whispers stir the silent night,
While the stars shine, pure and bright.

Footprints fade, the world still waits,
In the chill, enchantment radiates.
Glimmers caught in icy streams,
Reflecting all our gentle dreams.

Trees adorned in silver lace,
Nature wears a timeless grace.
Every shadow tells a tale,
Within the night, we sail, we sail.

Fragments of light, a frosty sheen,
Painting worlds in tranquil green.
In shimmering shadows, secrets grow,
Guiding hearts where lovers go.

In this hush, our spirits rise,
Chasing visions, star-kissed skies.
Hold this beauty, let it stay,
Shimmering shadows lead the way.

Starlit Frigid Expanse

In the night, the starlit dream,
Frigid air, a silvery beam.
Whispers echo in the dark,
As the winter sings its spark.

Across the vast, the cold winds sigh,
Blankets of snow, a gentle cry.
Every flicker, every gleam,
Fills our hearts with hope, a theme.

Wander through this frozen maze,
Where the moonlight softly plays.
In this expanse, the silence speaks,
As winter's heart the longing seeks.

Stars cascade like fallen seeds,
Nurturing our hidden needs.
In the depth of night we find,
A starlit expanse, intertwined.

So let us tread where dreams take flight,
In this magical, wondrous night.
Let every love beneath these skies,
Shine forever, light up our eyes.

Sunlit Snowfall

Softly the snowflakes drift and dance,
Glistening under the golden glance.
Whispers of winter in the gentle glow,
A dreamlike scene in a world of snow.

Each flake a story, unique and bright,
Painting the earth in purest white.
Sunlight sparkles on the frozen ground,
In this serene beauty, peace is found.

Children's laughter fills the chilly air,
Joy of the season, a moment rare.
Snowmen rise tall, with carrots for noses,
In this magical world, winter composes.

Footprints weave paths through the pristine white,
Chasing the sun in its winter flight.
Nature's canvas, a breathtaking sight,
Wrapped in the warmth of soft, pale light.

As evening falls on this snowy scene,
A hush of silence, serene and clean.
Stars peek out, one twinkle at a time,
In the quiet night, the world feels sublime.

Icy Specter

In the shadowed woods, a chill takes form,
An icy specter, where the cold winds swarm.
Frost clings to branches like a frozen sigh,
Whispers of winter as the night draws nigh.

Its gaze, a glimmer in the moon's soft light,
Threads through the darkness, haunting the night.
Ghostly figures dance upon the frozen lake,
Ethereal motion, as the cold winds shake.

Silent and haunting, it glides through the trees,
Carving harsh crystals in the wake of the breeze.
Echoes of time in this winter's chill,
Captured by shadows, forever still.

As dawn approaches, the specter's sway fades,
Leaving behind only ice-laden glades.
A memory lingers in the soft morning light,
A reminder of beauty in haunting fright.

In the heart of winter, where spirits roam,
Echoes of shadows find their way home.
Every snowy whisper tells tales of yore,
Of the icy specter and the legends it bore.

Eternal Winter's Light

A twilight glow in the longest night,
Hints of warmth in the fading light.
Eternal winter holds the world in grace,
Time stands still in this frozen space.

Snowflakes gather, a delicate swirl,
Nature's whisper in a cold, soft twirl.
Branches bow low with their weight of white,
Wrapped in the hush of the starry night.

Moonlight dapples the silent ground,
Soft as a prayer, a delicate sound.
Shadows play gently on the crystal snow,
A peaceful melody in the world below.

Hope blooms bright in the heart's quiet core,
For springtime whispers behind winter's door.
But for now, we bask in this gentle fight,
Forever enshrined in winter's light.

As the seasons turn, we hold on tight,
To the magic woven in eternal night.
For every cold dawn that follows still,
Is a promise of warmth, an unspoken thrill.

Frozen Dawn's Embrace

Awake to the glow of a frozen dawn,
Where frost-kissed petals drape the lawn.
A gentle embrace of the morning's breath,
Cocooned in silence, brushed by death.

Icicles glisten like silver threads,
Hanging from rooftops, where warmth once spread.
The world dressed in coats of shimmering lace,
In the soft light of dawn, a magical place.

Birdsong timidly breaks through the cold,
Notes of a story waiting to be told.
Nature awakens with a delicate grace,
In the beauty of winter's serene embrace.

Each moment lingers, wrapped in pure light,
As shadows retreat, giving way to bright.
A promise of life in the icy display,
In the frozen dawn where the night meets the day.

So let us wander in this tender glow,
Embrace the chill that whispers low.
For in every dawn, both frozen and warm,
Lies a world of wonder, a heart to transform.

In the Stillness of Cold

Whispers echo through the night,
Snowflakes dance in muted light.
Branches bow beneath the weight,
Nature's breath, December's fate.

Stars above, a twinkling choir,
Fires crackle, hearts inspire.
Chill descends, a solemn hush,
In the stillness, time is lush.

Footsteps crunch on frozen ground,
In this peace, deep dreams are found.
Frosted windows frame the scene,
Winter's beauty, pure and serene.

Blankets soft of white and gray,
Wrap the world in a gentle sway.
Every sigh a frosty plume,
In the cold, a whispered bloom.

Yet beneath the icy breath,
Lies the promise, life from death.
Spring will come, but for now,
We embrace the quiet vow.

Dim Ember in Freeze

A single flame flickers low,
In the night, a shadow's glow.
Chill surrounds, yet warmth remains,
A heart's pulse amidst the pains.

Timid light in winter's breath,
Holds its ground against cold death.
Whispered hopes in ember's core,
Glowing softly, longing for more.

Frosted glass and silent night,
Dimmed reflections, lost from sight.
Yet within, a spark persists,
In the freeze, a warmth exists.

As the moon spills silver beams,
Through the darkness, warmth redeems.
Against the frost, the ember fights,
Carrying dreams through coldest nights.

In the depth of winter's grip,
With each flicker, spirits lift.
Hope ignites though shadows creep,
In the still, the heart will leap.

Celestial Frost Patterns

Patterns swirl on windowpanes,
Nature's art, like soft refrains.
Fractal shapes and glistening trails,
In the quiet, beauty prevails.

Stars peek through the frosted veil,
Whispering secrets in the gale.
Celestial dance in icy lines,
Woven stories, nature's signs.

Every leaf, a frozen map,
Delicate as dreams that nap.
Contours trace the night's embrace,
In the cold, we find our place.

Underneath the starry sky,
Frosted beauty, soft and shy.
Glimmers shine from every spark,
In the stillness, waits the dark.

Though the chill may grip the world,
Every flake, a tale unfurled.
In the frost, we glimpse divine,
Nature's canvas, pure and fine.

Icicles of Dusk

Hanging low from rooftops' edge,
Icicles form a crystal hedge.
Glistening under twilight's kiss,
Each shard a moment not to miss.

Daylight fades to muted blue,
Still and calm, the darkness grew.
Nature's jewels catch the light,
Reflecting dreams of coming night.

A cascade of frozen tears,
Whispers echo from the years.
In the dusk, a silence stands,
Ice like glass in gentle hands.

Shadows stretch across the ground,
In the chill, serenity found.
Icicles dance in the fading sun,
A winter story just begun.

With each drop that falls in time,
A symphony, a quiet rhyme.
Dusk enfolds with gentle grace,
In the stillness, we find our place.

Snow-Kissed Glow

Gentle flakes fall from the sky,
Wrapping the world in a soft sigh.
The earth adorns a blanket white,
A tranquil scene, pure and bright.

Footprints dance in the fresh, soft snow,
Whispers of winter begin to flow.
Stars twinkle down on the silent ground,
In this stillness, magic is found.

Heartbeats quiet, the world takes pause,
Nature rests, without than a cause.
Branches heavy with glistening frost,
In this frozen realm, we are not lost.

Snowflakes twirl, a delicate waltz,
Each unique, like our dreams and faults.
The air is crisp, the night is near,
In this moment, nothing to fear.

As dawn unfolds, the sun breaks through,
Colors ignite in a vibrant hue.
The snow-kissed glow, a fleeting thrill,
A winter's beauty, timeless and still.

Elysium in Ice

A world encased in crystal dreams,
Where whispers float on winter's beams.
Frozen rivers twist and glide,
In this realm, beauty won't hide.

Glistening trees stand tall and proud,
Cloaked in ice, beneath a cloud.
Each branch a sculptor's work divine,
Nature's canvas, a perfect sign.

The moonlight dances on the sea,
Like silver threads in harmony.
The night reveals a ghostly glow,
In this paradise of frost and snow.

Voices of the wind softly sing,
Through valleys where enchanted dreams spring.
Elysium waits in winter's grasp,
A moment cherished, meant to last.

As dawn creeps in, a blush of gold,
The icy wonders never grow old.
A fleeting dream in winter's chill,
An Elysium, quiet and still.

Chilling Luminescence

In the stillness of the frozen night,
Stars spill forth their shimmering light.
A world transformed by chilly grace,
Where shadows dance, we find our place.

Echoes carry on the breeze,
Secrets shared among the trees.
Each crystal flake, a story told,
Of winter's grasp, a heart of gold.

Moonbeams kiss the icy ground,
In this tranquility, peace is found.
A chilling light, luminescent tease,
Whispers of winter in the trees.

Dreams drift softly on the air,
With every breath, a frozen prayer.
Beauty captured in this frigid realm,
Nature's wonders at the helm.

As dawn appears with a golden hue,
The world awakens, fresh and new.
Chilling luminescence fades away,
Yet echoes linger, here to stay.

Wraith of Radiant Chill

A specter glides through the silent night,
Wrapped in whispers, veiled in light.
The wraith of chill, with frosty breath,
Dances on the edges of winter's depth.

Its twinkling gaze, a deep azure,
In its presence, hearts feel pure.
A fleeting touch, a shiver's thrill,
Awakens dreams, so soft, so still.

Each breath of wind carries a sigh,
As the wraith drifts softly by.
Through silver meadows, across still lakes,
A radiant chill that never breaks.

Ghostly trails of shimmering dust,
In this enchanting realm we trust.
The wraith invites us to join the play,
Embracing the cold in a whimsical way.

As dawn awakens, the vision fades,
Leaving prints in the snowy glades.
The wraith of chill, a flicker of night,
In our hearts, its radiance alight.

Frost-Kissed Reverie

In the hush of the frosty night,
Whispers of dreams take their flight.
Stars twinkle in a velvet sky,
As the world breathes a soft sigh.

Moonlight dances on silver trees,
Carried by a gentle breeze.
Each flake tells a story untold,
In the magic of winter's hold.

Crystal patterns on window glass,
Time slows down as moments pass.
A warm fire crackles so bright,
Chasing away the chill of night.

Footsteps crunch on the frozen ground,
Echoes of joy in silence found.
Wrapped in cozy layers of wool,
Hearts are light, and spirits full.

So let this frosty dream unfold,
A canvas of white, a tale retold.
In every breath, in every sigh,
Frost-kissed reveries drift by.

Snow-Cloaked Glow

Softly falls the snow at dusk,
A blanket of peace, a gentle husk.
The world transforms in silver light,
Embracing the calm of the night.

Trees wear coats of white and gray,
Whispers carried in a frosty sway.
Footprints leading to dreams unbound,
In the silence, warmth is found.

Snowflakes twirl like dancers free,
Painting tales on the winter tree.
Each shimmer holds a fleeting glance,
Of the wonder within winter's dance.

Fires crackle with a golden hue,
As laughter echoes, warm and true.
Together we share this glowing sight,
In the heart of a snowy night.

Wrapping the world in a soft embrace,
Moments linger, lost in space.
In the quiet, the magic flows,
Underneath the snow-cloaked glow.

Twilit Cascade

As day surrenders to night's caress,
A cascade of colors, nature's dress.
Shadows dance in the fading light,
Whispers of stars begin their flight.

Rivers shimmer with a golden gleam,
Reflecting the hues of a twilight dream.
Echoes of dusk blend soft and low,
In the gentle sway of twilight's flow.

Mountains stand with a silent grace,
Holding the secrets of this place.
Time slows down with every sigh,
Underneath the vast, sprawling sky.

A chorus of crickets takes their stand,
As night weaves its stories, hand in hand.
In the quietude, hearts find peace,
In this twilit cascade, all worries cease.

Moments linger, like a soft embrace,
Lost in the beauty of twilight's space.
As day bows out to the night's cascade,
In the twilight's glow, memories are made.

Luminary Abyss

In the deep of night, stars ignite,
A luminary abyss, pure delight.
Galaxies swirl in a cosmic dance,
Inviting hearts to take a chance.

Nebulas whisper of the unknown,
In this darkness, dreams are sown.
Every twinkling light a beacon bright,
Leading souls through endless night.

Moonbeams spill across silent seas,
Carrying secrets on a gentle breeze.
With every glance, the heavens call,
In their embrace, we feel so small.

Luminous tales unfold with grace,
In the vastness, we find our place.
Eyes fixed upon the endless sky,
As the night deepens, we feel alive.

In the abyss where wishes soar,
Hope rekindles, forevermore.
With each heartbeat, the cosmos sings,
In the luminary abyss, the heart takes wing.

Daylight's Fray

Sunrise spills upon the land,
Whispers of a day just begun.
Shadows dance as soft winds strand,
Morning light ignites the sun.

Children laugh as they run free,
Chasing dreams beneath the glow.
Nature sings its jubilee,
In daylight's warm, embracing flow.

Clouds drift slow in skies so blue,
Birds take flight, a joyful sound.
Each moment paints a golden hue,
In daylight's opulent surround.

Yet shadows lurk, as daylight wanes,
Fading rays bring evening's peak.
Amidst the dusk, a hint of chains,
A reminder of what we seek.

As twilight wraps the world in grey,
Stars emerge to light the way.
In the night, we find our play,
A dance within daylight's fray.

Radiant Freeze

Frost captures the morning glow,
Crystals glisten on silence pure.
Nature holds its breath in snow,
A tranquil world, so majestically sure.

Branches wear their icy lace,
Every step an echo loud.
In this stark, enchanting place,
Winter wraps us in its shroud.

A frozen river glides so slow,
Reflections dance in chilly air.
The stillness spreads, a perfect show,
Radiance caught in winter's snare.

Bitter winds may softly sigh,
Yet warmth blooms in heart's retreat.
Underneath the leaden sky,
Hope shines bright, unceasing heat.

So embrace this frosty state,
As beauty weaves its frozen tease.
In the cold, we contemplate,
A world alive in radiant freeze.

Glare in Winter's Clutch

The sun's sharp glare upon the snow,
A dazzling light that blinds and stuns.
In winter's grasp, the cold winds blow,
While nature rests from summer's runs.

Each step, a crunch beneath our feet,
Soft flakes twirl like fairy dreams.
Time halts in this chill retreat,
As frosty whispers steal our gleams.

With every breath, the icy air,
Carves patterns that swirl in the light.
In winter's clutch, there's beauty rare,
Underneath the sun so bright.

We wander through this frozen maze,
Wrapped in layers, safe and warm.
Finding joy in winter's gaze,
Amidst the snow, the softest charm.

But shadows loom as daylight fades,
Stars emerge as twilight's pledge.
In winter's clutch, we hold our grades,
Finding peace on the ledge.

So let us cherish this cold embrace,
For in its heart, a glow resides.
In winter's glare, we find our place,
Where laughter and warmth collide.

Shivering Horizon

The edge of night greets the day,
Colors bleed in a gentle sigh.
Horizons stretch in twilight's play,
As whispers of the stars float by.

A shiver runs through silent trees,
Beneath the cloak of evening's rise.
Softly rustling with the breeze,
Nature calls as daylight dies.

In this transition, magic brews,
Where shadows stretch and softly creep.
Each moment offers varied hues,
A promise made, a secret keep.

The moon awakens with a grin,
Casting silver on sleeping ground.
A shivering pulse, the world within,
In twilight's grasp, all is unbound.

So let us linger on this edge,
Where dusk and dawn entwined, they dance.
In shivering light, a fleeting pledge,
To seize the moment, a daring chance.

As stars ignite the velvet sky,
We breathe in dreams from far and wide.
On the shivering horizon, we fly,
With hope held close, our hearts as guide.

Frozen Echoes

In the stillness of the night,
Whispers dance on silver light,
Time stands still, a breath in freeze,
Memories glide like fragile leaves.

Silhouettes of dreams long past,
Echo softly, shadows cast,
A frozen world, serene and bright,
Shimmers softly in the night.

A heart that knows the chill of change,
Finds beauty in the vast and strange,
Frosted branches, brittle break,
Nature's art, the silence wakes.

Silent songs of winter's song,
Tales of where the souls belong,
Echoes linger, sweet but cold,
Tattered stories left untold.

Frozen echoes, time will weave,
In every breath, a chance to grieve,
Yet in this peace, the heart will find,
The sacred bond of space and time.

Eclipsed by Winter's Breath

Frosted windows, morning light,
Casts a spell of pure delight,
Each breath dances, misty trails,
Frozen visions, winter pales.

Trees adorned with diamonds bright,
Underneath the pale moonlight,
Nature whispers, secrets kept,
In the silence, dreams have leapt.

Cold winds weave through every lane,
Carrying a sweet refrain,
Echoes of the past that linger,
Touched by time's elusive finger.

Eclipsed by winter's quiet grace,
Each falling snowflake finds its place,
A tapestry of white and blue,
In every flake, a world anew.

In this realm of frosted air,
We find solace, beyond despair,
Winter's breath, a calm embrace,
In the stillness, we find space.

Chilled Radiance

Beneath a sky of azure hue,
Radiance glimmers, soft and true,
Chilled whispers of the evening glow,
Paint the world in gentle snow.

Icicles hanging from the eaves,
Nature dons her crystal leaves,
Every sparkle tells a tale,
Of winter's breath on a silent gale.

Underneath the starlit sky,
Dreams rise up, a silent sigh,
Chilled radiance, warm embrace,
Fills the night's serene space.

A dance of light, both soft and pure,
In winter's heart, we find the cure,
For every shadow, there's a spark,
Illuminating the lingering dark.

In this stillness, we are whole,
Chilled radiance embraces the soul,
As snowflakes fall, a soft ballet,
Whispering peace in a wondrous way.

Glacial Glow

In a world wrapped tight in frost,
Moments captured, never lost,
Glacial glow, a radiant beam,
Frozen twilight, a fleeting dream.

Every flake a whisper low,
Painting tales in silence slow,
Branches bow with jeweled crowns,
In the hush, the magic drowns.

Echoes linger, silver bright,
Casting shadows in the light,
A landscape dressed in purest white,
Wonders flourish in the night.

From icy depths, a warmth will rise,
Fires that dance beneath the skies,
Glacial glow, a spark divine,
Uniting hearts, yours and mine.

In the chill, a warmth will swell,
Stories wrapped in winter's spell,
Glacial glow, a soft embrace,
Leaves us yearning for the grace.

Frosted Dawn

In quiet light, the world awakes,
A silver sheen on frozen lakes.
The whispers soft, like gentle breath,
Embrace the stillness, dance with death.

Frosted branches, jeweled and bright,
A canvas dressed in purest white.
The sun peeks through, a fleeting glance,
The day begins, a hopeful dance.

Crisp air carries the scent of pine,
Nature's wonders, oh how they shine!
Each step crunched underfoot today,
As winter wraps the world in play.

With every ray the shadows wane,
A gentle warmth, the chill's refrain.
Eager hearts await the thaw,
In Frosted Dawn, we find our law.

Ember Shadows on Snow

Flickering light on silken white,
Embers glow in the deep of night.
Casting shadows, a dance so slow,
An intimate waltz 'twixt warmth and snow.

Whispers of warmth in the biting air,
Silent secrets beyond compare.
Each spark a tale of days gone by,
Under starlit and endless sky.

The crackle sings a lullaby,
To dreams of summer, passing by.
While frost still lingers on the ground,
In ember's warmth, hope is found.

A fleeting moment, a heart's embrace,
In winter's arms, we find our place.
Ember shadows softly flow,
In the twilight of falling snow.

A Celestial Thaw

Beneath the vast and starry dome,
The frozen world begins to roam.
A gasp of warmth, a breath of spring,
The earth awakens, starts to sing.

Buds emerge from winter's hold,
Stories whispered, new and bold.
Gentle streams begin to flow,
In radiant hues, the flowers grow.

The ice melts back, revealing life,
In harmony, dispelling strife.
The sun, a lover, kisses ground,
In every heartbeat, joy is found.

Nature stretches, yawns and sighs,
As colors burst beneath clear skies.
A celestial thaw, pure and bright,
Gives birth to day from endless night.

Glistening Silence

In the quiet, a soft embrace,
Snowflakes fall, a delicate lace.
Crystals shimmer in twilight's gleam,
Wrapped in silence, we gently dream.

The world is hushed, the air so pure,
A moment held, we sit unsure.
Each breath we take, a ghostly sigh,
As tranquil nights float softly by.

The moonlight dances on frozen streams,
Guiding us through our quiet dreams.
Under starlit skies, we find peace,
In glistening silence, all worries cease.

The beauty whispers, soft and low,
A serene touch, a gentle glow.
In this stillness, hearts combine,
Lost together in glistening silence.

Gleam on Snowdrift

In the hush of winter's night,
A silver glow, pure and bright,
The world wrapped in a soft embrace,
Whispers dance, a gentle grace.

Footsteps muffled, silence deep,
Secrets that the moon will keep,
Stars above in quiet awe,
Nature's beauty, calm and raw.

Icicles hang with perfect form,
Chill that wraps the night so warm,
Each flake tells a tale unknown,
In the gleam, the truth is shown.

Branches glisten, diamonds sway,
Time stands still, the night holds sway,
A moment caught in timeless flow,
In the light's enchanting glow.

With dawn's kiss, the magic fades,
Yet the memory still cascades,
A fleeting charm of winter's art,
A gleam forever in the heart.

Echoes of a Chilled Dawn

Morning breaks with colors pale,
A wintry breath, the silence hails,
Echoes stir in frosty air,
Whispers float, soft as a prayer.

The world awakes, a fragile hue,
Glistening gems on grass anew,
Footsteps crunching in the dew,
Nature sings in tone so true.

Each shadow dances on the floor,
The light reveals what was before,
A canvas spread, the sun will paint,
Transform the chill with warmth so quaint.

Birds begin their morning song,
In perfect chorus, notes belong,
Harmony in every breath,
A cycle born from life and death.

The dawn unfolds with grace divine,
In every corner, pure design,
A fleeting moment, bright and clear,
Echoes of a dawn we hold dear.

Radiant Silence

Beneath a sky of softest gray,
Silence reigns at end of day,
A tranquil peace is all around,
In every heartbeat, whispers sound.

The ground is kissed by dying light,
Shadows stretch and fade from sight,
Stars awaken, one by one,
In the hush, their tales begun.

Moonlight spills on frozen streams,
Guiding dreams and secret themes,
Every ripple holds a sigh,
Fluid echoes drift and fly.

In this moment, still and vast,
The noise of life is left in past,
Radiant silence, pure and profound,
Cradles softly, wraps around.

Let time linger in the night,
Hold onto peace 'til morning's light,
For this quiet, sweet embrace,
Is a gentle, sacred space.

Napkin of Frost

Morning comes with a silver pen,
Writes stories on the earth again,
A napkin of frost, delicate lace,
Nature's artistry, a soft embrace.

Leaves adorned in glittering white,
Capturing dreams in early light,
Every blade, each petal holds,
A tale of winter softly told.

The world, a canvas painted fine,
Every contour, every line,
Once barren ground now sparkles bright,
In the hands of the morning light.

As time waits on this frosty veil,
Life awakens, a gentle trail,
The promise of warmth in every breath,
A dance with life, transcending death.

So let us marvel, pause and see,
The beauty in fragility,
For in every frost-tipped dawn so clear,
Lies the gentle whisper of the year.

Haloed in Winter's Breath

In silence draped, the frost descends,
The world a canvas, where beauty mends.
Each flake a whisper, soft and pure,
Embracing dreams, a gentle lure.

Beneath the stars, the shadows play,
As moonlight bathes the ground in gray.
A tranquil peace, the night bestows,
In winter's breath, the heart still glows.

Branches sparkling, diamonds hung,
Each frozen note, a song unsung.
In nature's hush, we find our way,
Through whispered winds, our spirits sway.

A halo formed, the world aglow,
With silver threads, the night weaves slow.
We walk in awe, as silence sings,
In winter's hold, the joy it brings.

So let us breathe this chilling air,
In every moment, peace we share.
Together wrapped in winter's song,
A wondrous night where we belong.

Aurora of the Chill

A canvas strewn with shades of blue,
As dawn awakens, crisp and new.
The chill of night begins to wane,
As colors dance, a sweet refrain.

The frost it glimmers, life in pause,
Nature rests without a cause.
A breathless hush, the moment's grace,
The world transformed, a warm embrace.

Soft hues unfold, the sky ignites,
With whispered secrets of starry nights.
Each ray a promise, soft and bright,
As daylight stretches, banishing night.

The icy breath begins to thaw,
As warmth unfurls a gentle draw.
In every hue, a story told,
In auroras painted, bright and bold.

So let us stroll through crisp air clear,
And greet the day with hearts sincere.
In every chill, a spark of light,
An aurora born from winter's night.

Twilight's Icy Veil

As day retreats, the twilight glows,
With icy tendrils, nature sows.
A veil of blue, the dusk unfolds,
As whispered secrets gently hold.

The shadows stretch, the stars appear,
A world transformed, so crystal clear.
With every breath, the silence grows,
In twilight's clutch, the magic flows.

The air electric, tinged with fate,
As winter's charm we contemplate.
Each flake of ice, a jewel rare,
A frozen dream suspended there.

We walk beneath the starlit dome,
In icy realms, we find our home.
Through every breath, a spell we cast,
In twilight's grasp, our hearts hold fast.

The night descends, yet still we shine,
In twilight's arms, our spirits entwine.
A moment caught in time's embrace,
In icy veil, we find our place.

Shattering Light of Winter

In crisp dawn's light, the world awakes,
With shattering beams, to night it breaks.
A glow ignites, the shadows flee,
As winter's song sets spirits free.

The landscape glimmers, a diamond sea,
Each frozen branch a symphony.
With every ray, the ice will melt,
A truth in light that we all felt.

Through frosty panes, the sunlight streams,
Awakening hope, igniting dreams.
Each beam a promise, soft and bold,
As winter's tale begins to unfold.

While winds may bite, our hearts remain,
In shattering light, we'll rise again.
Together bound, through cold we soar,
In every spark, love's endless war.

So take my hand, let shadows part,
With winter's glow, we'll warm the heart.
In every flicker, a chance to see,
The shattering light that sets us free.

Milton Keynes UK
Ingram Content Group UK Ltd.
UKHW010232111224
452348UK00011B/696